BIOMES

AND CLIMATE CHANGE

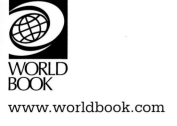

WORLD
BOOK

www.worldbook.com

For information about other World Book publications, visit our website at www.worldbook.com or call 1-800-WORLDBK (967-5325).

For information about sales to schools and libraries, call 1-800-975-3250 (United States) or 1-800-837-5365 (Canada).

World Book, Inc.
180 North LaSalle Street
Suite 900
Chicago, Illinois 60601
USA

The Library of Congress has catalogued an earlier edition as follows:
Title: Habitats and climate change.
Description: Chicago: World Book, a Scott Fetzer company, [2016] | Series: Earth's changing climate | Includes index.
Identifiers: LCCN 2015028045 | ISBN 9780716627081
Subjects: LCSH: Nature--Effect of human beings on--Juvenile literature. |
    Global environmental change--Juvenile literature. |
    Climatic changes--Juvenile literature. | Biogeography--Climatic factors--Juvenile literature.
Classification: LCC GF75 .C454 2015 | DDC 577.27--dc23
LC record available at http://lccn.loc.gov/2015028045

Reprinted as Biomes and Climate Change

This edition:
ISBN 978-0-7166-2768-5 (hc.)
ISBN 978-0-7166-2765-4 (set, hc.)

Also available as:
ISBN 978-0-7166-2776-0 (e-book)

Printed in China by Shenzhen Donnelley Printing Co., Ltd., Guangdong Province
3rd printing February 2019

Staff

Writers:
Edward Ricciuti
Echo Elise González

Executive Committee

President
Geoff Broderick

Vice President, Finance
Donald D. Keller

Vice President, Marketing
Jean Lin

Vice President, International Sales
Maksim Rutenberg

Vice President, Technology
Jason Dole

Director, Human Resources
Bev Ecker

Editorial

Director, New Print
Tom Evans

Managing Editor, New Print
Jeff De La Rosa

Editors
William D. Adams
Echo Elise González

Manager, Contracts & Compliance (Rights & Permissions)
Loranne K. Shields

Manager, Indexing Services
David Pofelski

Librarian
S. Thomas Richardson

Digital

Director, Digital Product Development
Erika Meller

Manager, Digital Products
Jonathan Wills

Manufacturing/ Production

Manufacturing Manager
Anne Fritzinger

Proofreader
Nathalie Strassheim

Graphics and Design

Senior Art Director
Tom Evans

Senior Designers
Matt Carrington
Isaiah Sheppard
Don Di Sante

Media Researcher
Rosalia Bledsoe

Senior Cartographer
John M. Rejba

Acknowledgments

Cover photo: © Anton Foltin, Shutterstock

Age footstock: 27 (Lightwave Photography). Alamy Images: 5 (blickwinkel), 15 (Norbert Probst/imageBROKER), 45 (Andy Holzman/ZUMA Press). AP Photo: 17 (Felix Marquez). Getty Images: 9 (Martin Harvey), 19 (John & Barbara Gerlach), 33 (Traumlichtfabrik). iStockphoto: 31 (Imagine Golf). Shutterstock: 7 (Adwo), 9 (Evenfh), 11 (Anna Gibiskys), 13 (Anita Kainrath), 23 (Daniela Constantinescu), 25 (tamapapat), 29 (Pi-Lens), 35 (Courtney A Denning), 37 (Trout), 43 (pzAxe). SuperStock: 39 (Dhritiman Mukherjee/age fotostock). U.S. Geological Survey: 21 (Ducks Unlimited), 41.

Table of contents

Glossary There is a glossary of terms on page 46. Terms defined in the glossary are in type **that looks like this** on their first appearance on any spread (two facing pages).

Introduction

A **biome** (BY ohm) is the collection of all living things in a large area of land or water. The boundaries of biomes are mainly based on geography and **climate.** Plants, animals, and other living things are all part of a biome.

Important land biomes of the world include forests, grasslands, tundra, and deserts. Each has its own combination of living things and its own special climate. Water biomes, such as oceans, bodies of fresh water, and **wetlands,** can be harder to define.

Each biome has an important role to play in keeping Earth's natural **cycles** and **ecosystems** balanced and healthy. For example, tropical rain forests add a huge amount of moisture to the **atmosphere.** This helps create rain in many other parts of the world. Many *species* (kinds) of plants and animals would not be able to survive outside of the biome in which they live. Even deserts provide important **habitat** for many of Earth's living things.

Increasing levels of **carbon dioxide** in the atmosphere are leading to rising global temperatures. These temperatures cause climate change, which affects biomes around the world. Most climate scientists agree that this rise in carbon dioxide is the result of human activities. This book discusses the effects that a changing climate has on Earth's biomes.

A scientist studies a **coral reef** on the ocean floor.

Global warming vs. climate change

People often use the terms *global warming* and *climate change* as if they are the same thing. In fact, these terms describe two different, but very closely linked, ideas. Global warming is the recent, rapid increase in the temperature of Earth's surface. This global increase in temperature is an average: not every place on Earth has warmed by the same amount, or even warmed at all. These uneven temperature changes have affected—and will continue to affect—such parts of the climate as yearly temperature highs and lows, **precipitation** totals, and how often **extreme weather** happens. These effects are together called *climate change*. Earth's climate has changed throughout its history, but the climate change brought on by human-caused global warming is unlike anything that has happened before.

Climate change and deserts

Compared to other **biomes,** the desert has few plants and animals. This is because it is very dry. Still, many different kinds of things live in Earth's deserts. Desert **ecosystems** are easily harmed. **Climate** change can easily upset the balance of plants and animals and the **habitat** on which they depend. Higher temperatures, for example, may spark more frequent wildfires that destroy desert plants, which grow so slowly they may never recover their place in the ecosystem.

A desert is dry because it does not receive enough rainfall to replace the water that evaporates. Scientists predict that global warming will cause rainfall in many deserts to decrease even more over the next 100 years. This could make it harder for desert life to get the water it needs.

Desert plants are producing more leaves. This shows that the amount of **carbon dioxide** in the air is increasing. Plants use carbon dioxide together with sunlight to make food and grow. However, the conditions causing increased leaf growth could cause other problems too. **Invasive** trees and shrubs that steal water used by desert plants and animals could take over habitats where they once could not survive.

The Valley of the Moon is in the Atacama Desert.

How are biomes, ecosystems, and habitats different?

Imagine a scorpion living in a rocky area of the Atacama Desert. It hides in the rocks and finds insects and small animals to eat. The scorpion relies on this rocky area for food and shelter. This means the rocky area is the scorpion's **habitat.** Rocks, sunlight, plants, animals, and many other living and nonliving things form the **ecosystem** of the Atacama Desert. This is one of the many ecosystems that make up all of Earth's deserts. The living things of all of these ecosystems combined make up the whole desert **biome.**

7

The Namib Desert

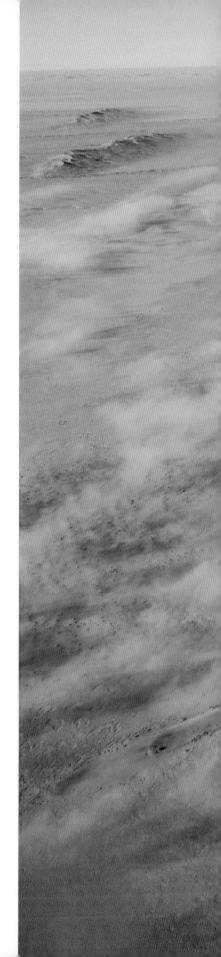

The Namib Desert is the oldest desert in the world. It measures about 100 miles (160 kilometers) across at its widest, and stretches 1,300 miles (2,080 kilometers) along the Atlantic coast in southwestern Africa. Though the Namib receives less than ¾ inch (2 centimeters) of rain a year, some areas have thick fog up to 180 days a year. Many living things depend on the precious moisture in this fog, which rolls in from the ocean.

Many living things make their home in the Namib Desert, including ostriches, cheetahs, moles, insects, and plants. Even elephants live in this desert. The strange *Welwitschia* (wehl WIHCH ee uh) plant, a short plant that grows only two leaves in its whole life, can only be found in the Namib.

However, global warming is causing the Namib Desert to become hotter and drier. Rising temperatures are threatening *Welwitschia* plants in the northern Namib. Some *Welwitschia* plants are thousands of years old, and scientists suspect that they might have already **adapted** to past changes in the **climate.** There is hope that, if warming does not increase too quickly, these plants may be able to adapt and survive. Other kinds of desert wildlife may not be so lucky.

The *Welwitschia* plant bears a single pair of leathery, green leaves that spread over the ground. Over time, hot winds, blowing sand, and age split the two leaves into long shreds.

Fog from the Atlantic Ocean rolls over the Namib Desert. Some plants and animals depend on the moisture from the fog to survive in this dry **habitat.**

Will deserts get bigger as Earth gets hotter?

Biomes that border deserts, such as grasslands, are threatened by a process called *desertification* (dehz UHR tih fih KAY shuhn). Desertification is the spread of a desert into a nearby biome. Human activities, such as farming, grazing livestock, and cutting down trees, *contribute* (add) to desertification.

More and more, **climate** change is also playing a role in desertification. Higher temperatures from global warming are drying out soils. Patterns of rainfall are changing, leaving some regions much drier. If this trend continues, the world's deserts will get larger.

The Sahara in Africa, the largest desert in the world, could expand far beyond its present borders. The Sahara covers 3.5 million square miles (9 million square kilometers) across the whole of northern Africa. In places, it is already spreading 30 miles (48 kilometers) a year, replacing valuable grasslands and *displacing* (forcing to move) the animals and plants that live there. The Gobi, a large desert in Asia, is also spreading south into farmlands in China. The Gobi is growing at up to 15.5 miles (25 kilometers) a year.

10

The ancient Sahara

The Sahara was not always a desert. Around 10,000 years ago, the Sahara was a green, grassy plain dotted with rivers and lakes. Elephants, hippopotamuses, and giraffes roamed the land. We know this because people living there long ago painted pictures of their surroundings on rocks. These people hunted and raised cattle, goats, and sheep. About 7,000 years ago, however, the rains began to drop off. The elephants, hippos, and giraffes disappeared. The people moved on. The Sahara turned into the world's largest desert.

Climate change and the ocean biome

Earth's oceans *absorb* (take in) **carbon dioxide** from the **atmosphere.** Animals breathe out this gas when their bodies change food into energy and living tissue. Carbon dioxide is also created by the burning of anything that has carbon in it. Such things include coal, gasoline, and wood.

When carbon dioxide reacts with seawater, the water becomes more **acidic.** In acidic waters, **calcium** gets broken down more easily. Some animals such as crabs and snails use calcium to build their shells. Waters that are highly acidic contain less calcium, which makes it harder for these animals to survive. Many fish and other creatures that eat these shell-building animals are also threatened because their food supply is in danger.

The ocean is becoming acidic at a very fast rate. Since the 1800's, people have released huge amounts of carbon dioxide into the atmosphere. Because the oceans continue to absorb that carbon dioxide, many scientists worry that *marine* (ocean) **ecosystems** will be badly harmed.

Many marine animals depend on sea grass to live.

The Great Barrier Reef

The Great Barrier Reef is off the coast of the state of Queensland in northeastern Australia. It spans about 1,400 miles (2,300 kilometers). It is not made of just a single **coral reef.** It is a system of almost 3,000 smaller reefs. The whole system is made up of some 400 different species of a marine animal called coral and their bony structures.

The Great Barrier Reef provides **habitat** for fish, dolphins, whales, sea turtles, sea grasses, and a great many other living things. It is home to about 1,500 species of fish alone. Many seabirds nest on the reef's 900 islands. But today, a one-two punch from **climate** change and direct human activities is threatening the Great Barrier Reef.

Higher water temperatures from global warming are causing many corals to force out the **algae** that lives in and feeds the coral. This is called *bleaching* because the coral turns white without its algae. Bleaching can kill corals. If a warm spell is temporary, corals may survive bleaching. In 1998, the highest sea temperatures ever recorded happened in the waters around the Great Barrier Reef. About half of the reef bleached.

Coral are also threatened by more **acidic** waters. Higher levels of acid in the water make it hard for coral to build their reefs. Experts worry that the Great Barrier Reef may not survive the effects of higher temperatures and ocean acidity.

Corals of the
Great Barrier Reef,
off the coast of
Australia

Protecting the reef

The Great Barrier Reef Marine
Park was established by the
nation of Australia in 1975. Much
of the park is off-limits to fishing.
No-fishing zones actually benefit
fishing in the oceans. Fish that
reproduce (make more living
things like themselves) under
protection help restock nearby
fishing areas.

15

Dead zones in the ocean

Global warming causes ocean waters to rise in temperature. Warm water does not hold as much **oxygen** as cold water. As the ocean warms, areas that have no oxygen, called *dead zones*, are forming in the waters. Low-oxygen zones happen naturally in oceans and in fresh water. They sometimes happen as a result of a weather pattern called *El Niño* (ehl NEEN yoh), which can cause certain areas of the ocean to become temporarily warmer. Human activities are reducing the oxygen in these zones even more, and are causing them to expand. Most living things cannot survive in a dead zone.

Water **pollution** is another cause of dead zones. Farms and factories can produce *land runoff*, waste and toxins that are spilled or washed into rivers and streams and end up in the ocean. Such pollution can cause *algae blooms* (huge populations of **algae** that grow quickly). This creates an imbalance in the ocean **ecosystem** that can turn the water into a dead zone.

The Earth's dead zones have grown four times in size since the year 1950. In fact, oxygen levels are dropping in all ocean waters. Scientists suspect that both water pollution and **climate** change are to blame.

A fisherman walks on a beach covered with dead sardines in Chile. Warm water temperatures from an unusually strong El Niño event caused a huge algae bloom, which killed these sardines and many other fish. Scientists think climate change may have worsened the effects of this El Niño event.

Climate change and freshwater biomes

Climate change can severely affect lakes, rivers, **wetlands,** and other freshwater **biomes.** Higher temperatures can upset the fragile **ecosystems** of these bodies of water. Shallow freshwater wetlands, such as swamps and marshes, are perhaps most easily harmed. They dry up fastest during **drought.**

Warming temperatures and water **pollution** can trigger **algae** blooms in lakes. Too many algae block sunlight from reaching deeper into the water. Algae that live deeper in the water do not receive enough sunlight and die. As the *remains* (dead bodies) break down, they aborb oxygen from the water. Fish species that need much oxygen, such as trout, die. Other fish that are able to live in low-oxygen waters, such as carp, take over. This sets off a chain of changes that upsets the whole ecosystem of the lake.

In some areas, climate change can lead to **extreme weather,** such as powerful hurricanes or huge amounts of rain that can cause floods. Wind and floodwaters carry soil and pollution into bodies of fresh water. The pollution can harm wildlife as well as the humans who drink that water. Some freshwater species are threatened by the added soil. For example, soil-clogged streams can prevent salmon from reproducing.

A Canada goose rests in a freshwater pond filled with green algae.

The Prairie Pothole region

The **wetland** is one of the most threatened **biomes** in the world today. Wetlands are areas of land where the ground remains soaked for most of the year. They face a number of serious threats, including **pollution** and the spread of **invasive** species. People have drained many wetlands in order to build their homes or businesses on that land. **Climate** change also threatens wetlands around the world.

The Prairie Pothole region of North America covers more than 300,000 square miles (800,000 square kilometers) from the U.S. state of Iowa to the province of Alberta in Canada. More than half of North America's **migrating** water birds depend on this region to reproduce, feed, or take shelter for part of the year. This region is sometimes called "America's duck factory."

Potholes are shallow, low areas in the **prairie** that fill with snow and rainwater. Many scientists predict that global warming could cause longer and more severe **droughts** that could dry up the potholes. Changing weather is already making western parts of the Prairie Pothole region hotter and drier. The eastern potholes are expected to have cooler, wetter weather. However, farming has claimed most potholes there. The loss of potholes would greatly reduce many populations of North American ducks.

Prairie Pothole region

Ice age relics

Ice age **glaciers** covered the pothole region until about 10,000 years ago. The potholes formed when advancing glaciers scraped *depressions* (pits) into the earth. As the glaciers *retreated* (melted back), they filled the depressions with fresh water. Each year the potholes refill with rain and snowmelt.

Freshwater biomes and sea-level rise

Global warming is causing the **sea level** to rise. Sea level is the level of the ocean's surface. As Earth's **atmosphere** warms, **glaciers** and other forms of land ice melt. The water from this melting ice seeps into the ocean, adding to the *volume* (amount of space taken up) of the ocean's water. The rising temperature of the ocean itself causes the water to *expand* (take up more space), which causes the sea level to rise even more.

As sea levels rise, freshwater **ecosystems** are increasingly in danger of being *contaminated* (soiled) by salt water. Most plants and animals that live in fresh water cannot survive in *high-salinity* (salty) waters. But unlike other living things whose **habitats** are changing, they cannot usually move away to a better habitat. They are often stuck in the body of water in which they live.

Many marshes, swamps, and bodies of fresh water all around the world are increasingly threatened by rising sea levels.

Magpie geese rest in the waters of the Corroboree Billabong in Australia's Mary River Wetlands. Sea-level rise threatens many of the **wetlands** where geese, kingfishers, cormorants, and other freshwater birds nest and find food.

23

Climate change and forests

A forest is an area of land covered with trees. Each forest plant and animal has *evolved* (changed over generations) to fit into its particular *environment* (surroundings).

For example, oak trees have evolved to be *fire resistant*. They have thick bark and other features that protect them from fire. Many animals of the oak forest, such as salamanders, have **adapted** to forest fires by going to water or burying themselves underground when fire is near. When fire spreads across an oak forest, it kills **invasive** plants and animals. But the oak trees and other fire resistant plants and animals are able to survive. In this way, fire can help the native wildlife thrive.

But heat and **drought** from **climate** change cause more intense forest fires. The extreme temperatures can be deadly even for fire resistant living things. Global warming can also make forest fires occur more often. This can be particularly damaging to *boreal* forests (forests found in cold climates), which take a long time to recover after a fire.

Climate change can upset the balance of forest **ecosystems** in many ways. Extreme storms can create stronger-than-normal winds that knock over trees. Changes in rainfall and temperature can make forest **habitats** less suitable for native wildlife and more suitable for invasive species.

Different kinds of forests

There are three major kinds of forest **biomes.** They are the *tropical*, *temperate*, and *boreal* forests. The main difference between them is **climate.** One example of this difference is temperature. Tropical forests have the hottest average yearly temperatures, while boreal forests have the coldest temperatures. Temperate forests, such as oak forests, have both hot summers and cold winters. Climate change affects each of these biomes in different ways.

El Yunque rain forest

Rain forests are woodlands that grow in areas with plenty of rain. The rain forest **biome** covers less than 3 percent of Earth. Yet it is home to more than half of all plant and animal species.

El Yunque (ehl YOONG keh) tropical rain forest is located on the Caribbean island of Puerto Rico. Many small animals, such as bats, birds, lizards, frogs, fish, and insects live in El Yunque. It is also home to many kinds of plants, such as trees, ferns, and orchids.

Climate change is threatening El Yunque in various ways. The number of *arthropods* living in El Yunque today is as much as 60 times lower than it was in the 1970's. Arthropods are animals that have jointed legs and no backbone, such as insects, spiders, and crabs. Scientists have found that rising temperatures are the main force behind this reduced number. Many populations of birds, lizards, and other animals that eat the arthropods are also decreasing.

In 2017, Hurricanes Irma and Maria struck Puerto Rico, knocking out electric power throughout the island and causing much damage. Thousands of people died as a result. El Yunque's **ecosystem** also took a blow. Powerful winds and heavy rains knocked down many trees and caused landslides. The hurricanes killed wildlife and destroyed much of their forest **habitat.** Scientists have linked the *severity* (harshness) of Hurricane Maria to climate change.

Running out of time

The Puerto Rican parrot, also called the *iguaca* (ih GWAH kuh), is a critically **endangered** parrot living in El Yunque rain forest. Iguacas have been threatened by such human activities as hunting and forest clearing for many years. Today, **extreme weather** caused by climate change is another serious threat to this species. In 2017, powerful hurricanes killed many iguacas, while destroying a large number of the trees that they rely on for food and shelter. More than half of the population of iguacas disappeared after the hurricanes. Scientists worry that, like countless other rain forest animals, the iguaca may soon go **extinct.**

How do forests adjust to climate change?

Global warming is changing the location of forest **biomes** on Earth. Trees are now growing on the southern edges of the normally treeless tundra in northern Canada (see page 36). Now, boreal forests, made up of spruces, firs, and other *conifers* (trees with needles and cones), are spreading into the thawing tundra as the **climate** grows warmer. These trees can survive in cold—but not frozen—ground.

Although it is advancing over tundra, Canada's boreal forest is not expanding to cover more land. Its southern boundary is also moving northward. The entire forest is shifting toward the north because of global warming. Temperatures at the southern part of the forest are becoming too warm for conifers. Grasslands are taking over that land.

By 2100, forest near the province of Alberta, in Canada, may shift 100 miles (160 kilometers) north. But, individual trees cannot move. Tree species rely on the movement of their seeds to shift their range northward. This takes a long time. Some species of trees may go **extinct** because they cannot keep up in this race against climate change.

Boreal forest in
Yukon, Canada

Climate change and grasslands

Grasslands—open areas of grassy land with few trees—cover huge portions of Earth's surface. Grasslands grow well in areas that receive about 10 to 40 inches (25 to 100 centimeters) of rain each year. Less rain results in desert, while more rain supports forests.

Natural wildfires, seasonal **drought,** and grazing by large animals are all important parts of grassland **ecosystems,** in part because they kill tree *saplings* (young trees). Grassland plants, on the other hand, have **adapted** to these conditions. This stops forests from invading grasslands.

Human activities, such as farming and raising livestock, have already done great damage to many grasslands around the world. **Climate** change is another threat to the grassland **biome.** Global warming has increased wildfires and drought, giving grasses less time to recover. In some areas, changing wind patterns bring more rainfall, so shrubs and trees begin to replace grasses. Increased **carbon dioxide** in the **atmosphere,** a result of human activities, also helps these larger plants to take over grasslands.

Many grasslands have already been lost because of human activities. Now, climate change threatens to turn much of the grassland biome into desert or forest. If the grassland biome is lost, many important plants and animals will go **extinct.**

Prairie plants flower in the U.S. state of Washington. The prairie was once a sea of grass that covered much of North America. Most of it has been replaced by buildings and farmland, such as that seen in the background here. Today, less than 1 percent of the original North American prairie remains.

African savannas

The *savanna* is a grassland with widely scattered trees and shrubs. Many kinds of flowering plants grow among savanna grasses. Savannas cover more than two-fifths of Africa and large areas of Australia, India, and South America. They are also found in some parts of North America.

The baobab (BAY oh bab) tree is an African savanna tree that has a very thick trunk, which can grow more than 100 feet (30 meters) around. It is sometimes called the "upside-down tree" because its branches look like roots.

The baobab is a very important part of the **ecosystem** of the African savanna. Many animals live in the tree's branches and trunk, eat its fruits, or drink nectar from its flowers. The baobab is perfectly **adapted** to survive its very dry environment. Its thick bark holds lots of water, and its long roots can find underground water even during **droughts.** Like other savanna trees, baobabs are able to survive grassland fires.

Baobabs can live for thousands of years, but since 2005 many have begun to die. Scientists do not yet know why they are dying, but studies show that increased drought and rising temperatures are partly to blame. This means that **climate** change is likely leading to baobab deaths.

A baobab tree grows among savanna shrubs and grasses in Tanzania's Tarangire National Park.

Why are grasslands important?

Grasslands support huge populations of plants and animals. Sixty million bison, also called American buffalo, once roamed the grasslands of North America. Adult bison eat about 60 pounds (27 kilograms) of grass each day. But a healthy grassland can handle this. Bison might be able to survive in forest **habitats,** but only in much smaller numbers. There is simply not enough food for them in the forests.

Wide-open grasslands provide ideal habitat for birds that hunt by sight. **Prairie** falcons chase small birds at high speeds close to the ground. Trees and large shrubs would interfere with the falcon's hunting.

Many grassland plants need lots of sun. They could not survive in the shade of trees. Many animals depend on these plants for food.

The grassland **biome** is also an important *carbon sink*. A carbon sink is a natural area that absorbs more **carbon dioxide** from the **atmosphere** than it produces. Forests store carbon dioxide inside the wood and leaves of trees, which means that wildfires release it back into the atmosphere. But grassland plants store carbon dioxide in their roots and in the soil, where fire cannot release them. This makes the grassland a reliable and important carbon sink as the **climate** changes.

A bumble bee collects pollen
and nectar from a prairie flower.

Tundra and climate change

Tundra is a treeless **biome** where much of the ground is frozen. There are two types of tundra. *Alpine tundra* forms on high mountains. At such heights, temperatures are so low that the brief warm season is too short for trees to survive. *Arctic tundra* lies in the far north. This region near the North Pole experiences long, cold winters. Summer temperatures rarely climb above 50 degrees Fahrenheit (10 degrees Celsius). Trees cannot sink roots into *permafrost* (ground that stays frozen all year). Only low-lying plants and **lichens** (LY kuhnz) can survive here.

Only about 10 inches (25 centimeters) of **precipitation** (prih SIHP uh TAY shuhn), mostly snow, falls on tundra in a year. Even so, its surface gets soggy. Water pools and puddles on the permafrost. Swarms of mosquitoes thrive there. Large deer called caribou (KAR uh boo) dig through snow to feed on lichens and plants all year. Smaller animals **hibernate** during the bitterly cold winter.

But now global warming is threatening the tundra. Warmer temperatures are allowing some trees and other **invasive** plants and animals to move into the tundra, replacing the wildlife native to the area. Tundra plants and animals can move north where it is still very cold. But once they reach the Arctic Ocean, there is nowhere else to go. Alpine tundra wildlife can escape the warmth by moving higher, but it can only go as high as the mountain top.

Low plants are covered with snow and water begins to freeze as the long winter begins in the Alaskan tundra.

37

Himalayan alpine tundra

Alpine tundra is found on high mountains all over the world. It usually begins at about 10,000 feet (3,000 meters) above **sea level,** and higher on mountains closer to the equator. The boundary above which trees cannot grow is called the *tree line.*

In the Himalaya—mountains found in Bhutan, China, India, Nepal, and Pakistan—the tree line is around 12,000 feet (3,700 meters) high. Above that, only such small things as mosses, bushes, and **lichens** are able to grow. Even higher than the alpine tundra lies the *snow line.* Above this height, no plants or animals can make a home.

Many of the animals that live on lower slopes of the Himalaya also roam the alpine tundra. Mountain sheep and the Himalayan tahr, a relative of sheep and goats, are hunted by snow leopards. Brown bears and wolves also sometimes range high into this frozen **habitat.**

Today, **climate** change seems to be reducing the amount of **precipitation** in the Himalaya. As climate change continues, the frozen alpine tundra will eventually thaw. If rain and snow decrease and the land continues to thaw, the Himalayan tundra could become more like a desert, where few plants and animals can live.

A brief flowering

During the brief summer in the Himalaya of northern India, the alpine tundra springs to life with blooming flowers. These plants are largely *dormant* (not active) during the long winter when snow carpets the landscape.

The warming tundra

In the tundra, warming temperatures are perhaps the most worrisome part of **climate** change. Much global warming is caused by people burning **fossil fuels,** which increases the amount of **greenhouse gases** in the **atmosphere.** Greenhouse gases trap heat in the atmosphere, warming Earth.

But other things also contribute to global warming. One is the loss of snow cover in the tundra. Bright tundra snow and ice reflect sunlight back into space, so that sunlight does not warm Earth. If the snow melts, the darker soil underneath absorbs more sunlight and releases it as heat, warming the air.

The permafrost may be like a time bomb that is about to go off. Huge amounts of greenhouse gases have been trapped in Arctic tundra permafrost for thousands of years. These gases mostly come from the remains of plants that died long ago. When permafrost thaws, the gases are released into the atmosphere. This release speeds up warming in the region, causing even more thawing.

A block of thawing permafrost collapsed on the Arctic coast of Alaska, in the far northwestern United States.

Why are biomes important to humans?

The loss of natural areas and the wildlife that they support affects humans in ways almost beyond counting. Natural environments not only provide clean air, water, food, and scenic beauty, but also other benefits. For example, many important medicines are made from chemicals that were found in rain forest plants. Who knows what undiscovered benefits are waiting to be found in the rain forest and other **biomes?**

Forests recycle much of the water that becomes rain. The Amazon rain forest provides moisture to areas as far away as the midwestern United States. Without forests to recycle water, terrible **droughts** would be more widespread in many different biomes. When drought turns grasslands and other biomes into desert, people are at risk of starvation.

The **wetland** biome shields coastal communities from **storm surges** and floods by soaking up extra water. Almost 70 percent of people in the U.S. state of Louisiana live within 50 miles (80 kilometers) of the northern coast of the Gulf of Mexico. Without wetlands, millions of people are in greater danger from hurricanes and the damaging storm surges they bring.

Mangrove trees on Sri Lanka's coast send their stiltlike roots into the salty water. Mangroves help reduce the damage that tsunamis and tropical storms create in many coastal communities. But rising **sea levels** are threatening mangroves around the world.

How can we help save our biomes?

All people can help slow down **climate** change by changing little things in their everyday lives. If everybody does a little, it adds up to a big benefit for the natural world.

Producing electric power often involves burning such **fossil fuels** as coal and natural gas, which *emits* (releases) **carbon dioxide** and contributes to global warming. By reducing our use of electric power, we can help reduce the production of **greenhouse gases.**

Turn off computers and other electronic devices when no one is using them. Unplug phone chargers when electronic devices are not being powered up. Replace old light bulbs with energy-saving bulbs. Take shorter showers to save fuel used to heat water. Encourage your family to spend more time walking and less time driving. Many of these tips will also help save money.

Nature centers and conservation groups do more direct work to help preserve natural areas. Try to find a local nature center where you can visit or even volunteer. The centers will help you discover many different ways you can help protect and improve the natural areas around your home.

Helping out

Famed *naturalist* (nature expert) Jane Goodall founded Roots & Shoots, a program in which young people around the world help communities and animals, and work to protect natural environments. Roots & Shoots involves about 150,000 young people in more than 120 countries. Kids work with adult mentors to help preserve **habitats** in their own communities. For example, members have planted thousands of new trees across the United States. In Thailand, a project leader taught children about the "three R's"—reducing, reusing, and recycling—that help our environment.

45

GLOSSARY and RESOURCES

acidic High in acid. Acid is a substance *dissolved* in (spread out into) water that breaks down many kinds of materials.

alga (plural, algae) A simple living thing that can make its own food. Algae live in oceans, lakes, rivers, ponds, and moist soil.

adapt For a living thing to change in structure, form, or habits to fit different conditions.

atmosphere The mass of gases that surrounds a planet.

biome The collection of all living things in a large area of land or water. Geography and climate determine the boundaries of a biome.

carbon dioxide A gas that helps regulate Earth's temperature. Animals produce carbon dioxide and release it into the atmosphere. Plants use carbon dioxide from the atmosphere to live and grow.

climate The weather of a place averaged over a length of time.

coral reef A type of underwater structure largely made of a framework of limestone skeletons created by ocean animals called corals.

cycle The growth or actions that happen (in a special order) by which something goes through a set of changes. Usually, cycles repeat themselves, the end circling around to a beginning—for example, the seasonal cycle of spring, summer, fall, winter, then spring again.

drought When the average precipitation for an area drops far below the normal amount for a long time.

ecosystem A system made up of living things and their *environment* (surroundings).

endangered When a *species* (kind) of living thing is threatened with extinction.

extreme weather Any weather that is very unusual for a particular place or threatens to cause injuries, deaths, or great damage to crops and property.

extinct When every member of a *species* (kind) of living thing has died.

fossil fuel An energy-providing material—coal, oil, or natural gas—formed from the long-dead *remains* (bodies) of living things.

glacier A large mass of ice that moves slowly down a slope.

greenhouse gas Any gas that warms Earth's atmosphere by trapping heat.

habitat The kind of place in which a living thing usually lives.

hibernate To spend a season in an inactive, sleeplike state called *hibernation*.

invasive Spreading rapidly in a new environment. Invasive species are often harmful to the new environment.

lichen Any of a group of living things that consist of a fungus and a simple living thing, such as an alga, growing together in a single unit.

oxygen A gas that nearly all living things need to stay alive.

pollution Materials that *contaminate* (soil) and harm the natural environment.

prairie An area of flat or hilly land covered mainly by tall grasses.

precipitation Moisture in the form of rain, snow, sleet, ice, or hail.

sea level The level of the ocean's surface.

storm surge A sudden rush of waves onto land caused by strong winds.

wetland An area of land where the ground remains soaked with water for most of the year. Swamps, marshes, and bogs are wetlands.

Books:

Brundle, Harriet. *Habitat Destruction*. New York: KidHaven Pub., 2018.

Green, Dan, and Simon Basher. *Climate Change*. New York: Kingfisher, 2014.

Herman, Gail. *What Is Climate Change?* New York: Penguin Workshop, 2018.

Kurlansky, Mark, and Frank Stockton. *World without Fish*. New York: Workman Pub., 2014.

McPherson, Stephanie Sammartino. *Arctic Thaw: Climate Change and the Global Race for Energy Resources*. Minneapolis: Twenty-First Century Books, 2015.

Websites:

NASA – Climate Change and Global Warming
https://climate.nasa.gov/

National Park Service – Climate Change
https://www.nps.gov/subjects/climatechange/

United States Environmental Protection Agency – A Student's Guide to Global Climate Change
https://archive.epa.gov/climatechange/kids/index.html

United States Environmental Protection Agency – Climate Impacts on Ecosystems
https://archive.epa.gov/epa/climate-impacts/climate-impacts-ecosystems.html

Think about it:

Climate change is causing biomes to shift. The plants and animals on the edges of these biomes have to move or adapt to survive. In some areas, completely new ecosystems might appear where the shifts are happening. No one knows yet what these new ecosystems would be like.

What are some good and bad things that could happen as biomes shift? For example, if an area started turning from forest into desert, some tree species might not be able to move fast enough and they might die. But other trees might survive by adapting to the hotter, drier climate of the desert.

INDEX